then telling
be *the*

antidote

PREVIOUS WINNERS OF
THE BERKSHIRE PRIZE
Tupelo Press First / Second Book Award

Brandon Rushton, *The Air in the Air Behind It*
Selected by Bin Ramke

Iliana Rocha, *The Many Deaths of Inocencio Rodriguez*
Selected by Oliver de la Paz

Laurel Nakanishi, *Ashore*
Selected by Carl Phillips

Anna Marie Hong, *Fablesque*
Selected by Aimee Nezhukumatathil

Elizaabeth Acevedo, *Medusa Reads La Negra's Palm*
Selected by Gabrielle Calvocoressi

Patrick Coleman, *Fire Season*
Selected by Carol Frost

Jenny Molberg, *Marvels of the Invisible*
Selected by Jeffrey Harrison

Amy McCann, *Yes, Thorn*
Selected by Paisley Rekdal

Kristina Jipson, *Halve*
Selected by Dan Beachy Quick

Ye Chun, *Lantern Puzzle*
Selected by D.A. Powell

Mary Molinary, *Mary & the Giant Mechanism*
Selected by Carol Ann Davis and Jeffrey Levine

Daniel Khalastchi, *Manoleria*
Selected by Carol Ann Davis and Jeffrey Levine

Megan Snyder-Camp, *The Forest of Sure Things*
Selected by Carol Ann Davis and Jeffrey Levine

Jennifer Militello, *Flinch of Song*
Selected by Carol Ann Davis and Jeffrey Levine

Kristin Bock, *Cloisters*
Selected by David St. John

Dwaine Rieves, *When the Eye Forms*
Selected by Carolyn Forché

Lilias Bever, *Bellini in Istanbul*
Selected by Michael Collier

David Petruzelli, *Everyone Coming Toward You*
Selected by Campbell McGrath

Bill Van Every, *Devoted Creatures*
Selected by Thomas Lux

Aimee Nezhukumatathil, *Miracle Fruit*
Selected by Gregory Orr

Jennifer Michael Hecht, *The Last Ancient World*
Selected by Janet Holmes

WINNER of the BERKSHIRE PRIZE

"In *then telling be the antidote*, Xiao Yue Shan writes: 'Sometimes/we spoke in a language so heavy that we passed/the words around in our hands.' In this beautiful book of poems, Shan's language floats in the liminal space between countries, between history, between language. Shan's poems explore themes of home, gender, politics, all the while exploring the threshold of the long line. **These poems are lush and airy at once, uncertain and certain, powerful and gentle. Shan's voice is unique and her gifts palpable, and we're so lucky to have her words passed onto our hands.**"

— from the Judge's Citation by Victoria Chang

Xiao Yue Shan is a poet born in China and living on Vancouver Island. Her chapbook, *How Often I Have Chosen Love*, was published in 2019.

Tupelo Press
North Adams, Massachusetts

then telling *be* *the* antidote

POEMS   XIAO YUE SHAN

ISBN: 978-1-946482-92-1
Library of Congress Control Number: 2023932643

Cover photo: Shuling Guo, "Sotto Voce-Saint Pierre, Martinique 2," 2021.
Oil on canvas. © Shuling Guo. Courtesy of the artist.

*Cover and text designed and composed in Adobe Garamond
by Dede Cummings and Xiao Yue Shan.*

Tupelo Press
P.O. Box 1767, North Adams, Massachusetts 01247
(413) 664–9611 / editor@tupelopress.org / www.tupelopress.org

Tupelo Press is an award-winning independent literary press that
publishes fine fiction, nonfiction, and poetry in books that are a
joy to hold as well as read. Tupelo Press is a registered 501(c)(3)
nonprofit organization, and we rely on public support to carry out
our mission of publishing extraordinary work that may be outside
the realm of the large commercial publishers. Financial donations
are welcome and are tax deductible.

This project is supported in part by the
National Endowment for the Arts

CONTENTS

ACKNOWLEDGMENTS

thank you to the following journals and collections, in which these poems previously appeared:

the poetry review: "conjuring"; "the man I love ran off with everything except my poems"

kenyon review: "wealth distribution will not be considered in the economic reform"; "the right to work"; "kitchen"; "strategy"

no tokens: "a vision of tomorrow"

poetry: "in love as in tourism"; "details   escape"

cicada: "modals of lost opportunity"; "rises in the urban population determining that each resident be allotted 1.6 square meters of personal space"; "in beijing the young writers ask me why people always want to talk about censorship"

literary hub: "mong kok, october 2019"

wildness: "to talk with you"

best new poets: "the coming of spring in the time of martial law" *juxtaprose:* "search by no light"

hobart: "montreal I"

la piccioletta barca: "always the clock, always the corridor, always the staircase"

thank you also to the editors of frontier poetry, who published my debut chapbook, *How Often I Have Chosen Love*, in which some poems from this collection can also be found.

thank you to judge of the berkshire prize, victoria chang, for your generosity in selecting this manuscript.

thank you to shuling guo for her beautiful paintings. it is an honour to have her work for the cover.

thank you to my mother, zhang guan wei, and my father, shan lian quan. thank you for giving me the world. for making me brave. without your love there would be no poems.

a photograph of tomorrow

日

sunlight something you trap in a room

月

moonlight a ladder gasping downward

明

and so easily a minor infinity

striations

battered clouds. animal sky. tokyo
paints cubist, sending the day to us
in shards. tile, orange, porcelain.
dark glyphs of telephone wire
crafting inky pictures amidst
sangenjaya's low, silent roofs
as the underground stairway
shudders with the wet slippings
of steps. human currents
tiding toward the thinning alleys
in relief. bright ripples of speaking.
something burns the way only
night allows for, which is to say,
briefly imagined in the small cold,
while beautiful compact darkness
dapples light along as perfume.
now, I can say *then* as if it were
still. such is the heaven of images—
elements abiding their perfection.
the metro lines the pulse of setagaya,
you bring your feet up on the seat.
again the city's lattice blurs into
lace, time sets the slate for action,
and together we move horizontally
along the practiced methods of
steel. its machine way of voiding
motion. east on the map as
it approaches west on the clock.
we are heading home.

this city is how I find you
and I will never see you outside it.
the long way this land obeys
its shapely waters, it reminds me
how often beauty comes to resemble
surrender. like rhododendron, neon
taxi skids, bracing teeth of ivy.
crows getting fat and happy
on yellow rims of fried chicken
supple in paper, then slowly
taking flight as if falling upward.
I think of rexroth. was it that time *is*
the mercy of eternity, or time *at*
the mercy of eternity? past the hour
knitting greens together in rain,
we bend the last stalks of camellia
along higashiyama's short houses,
tracing what has moved and what
has been touched, lemon trees and
brooms supine in doors. you were
telling me that mountains in japan
expressed the verticality of space,
that their true height is inward at an
invisible centre. the pressing of
knowing into unseen places
is how one trains in that great art,
patience. not conquering outward
but tunneling within—streets
and the imagination of direction.

to live is to study the borders,
distance poured by the mind
to flood hidden forms. kenko
spoke about a man whose only
regret, upon death, was to have
left behind the sky. its dusky
efflorescence, silk, steam, grand
delusions of infinity, putting
our own lengthy promises to
shame. no one knows what to do
with all that vastness, anyway.
we'd go bad going on forever,
so the whole of history crowds
to sit at a single table, lighter
and shiftier and more prone
to questions. we speak to capture
all this that does not keep shape,
clasping its cindered shimmer
in diagrammed sentences,
our own lovely unaloneness.
the triangulation between you, I,
and the always possible nature
of a very next moment—that
is the doorway I would like to keep
walking through, seeking wonder
of the unmysterious kind, wherein
the distant and minute grows
larger and more daunting as one
unthinkingly approaches them.

we are used to pretending a certain
choice, like settling on land or tide
at the end of all these very long nights.
but no imagination goes to these
endings. it is a simple alignment that
leads the hair of botticelli's venus
to stir the lotus girl of *genka*. that
sends miłosz's reflections of clouds
and trees into the bare cherry
etching wild into meguro river.
we simply end up, as it seems,
soft in bathwater, tired in laundry,
our bodies fitting liquid shapes
washing through the minutes,
taking the brief by its single thread
and leading it passingly to the sea.
on, and on, and on. sometimes
I think my thinking has nothing
if not your head to hang to,
becoming suddenly afraid at leaving
the sky after already having formed
an entirety to fit beneath it.
you are sheltering the grace of
an eye that has seen endlessness,
in which my love, my remarks
on love, my noticings and slight
carbons are salvaged. you are what
I know, as I go and return from
the long landscape of knowing.

this is not the first place we've
called here, and you are not
the first to be searched for
amidst the long velvet sheets
of lyric, wandering towards music
during the quiet. clear and high
on whiskey and tan simmers
of salted fish, petalled along
rice squared in cedarwood, we
lay crosswise against the braided
tatami grain, and watch as
the sailing boundary between
your language and mine practices
its peaks and hallucinations,
geometries and theologies.
in this flawless staging of
immortality, the lover dreams,
disappears, survives passion's
interrogations, and the turning bird
of desire sings through the night.
there are always such ancient
questions, unyielding and
insistent, on this side of the wide
lateness. yet holding one another
we form some simple line where
they do not hesitate to land.
folding their wings. listening to silence.
asking nothing for a moment, which—
as I have told you—is for ever.

maps

at the intersection of desire I want to tear down the small house where I've lived a long time. terrifying the land, tracing tresses of demarcation. bearable longing of risk carrying itself to an essential condition. at the point of obliteration is the word yes, impossible gleaming syllable destabilizing the air like bodies shifting in dance, that one deep persistent instinct to feel first with beauty. to exclude the ugly distance between oneself and nothingness. I want my body to stay a body. I don't want it revealed as architecture, constitutions of willow-wood and heaven-will, vague orchards, glistening black stars of apple-seed. I want to stand at the very centre of something looking outward, at all this growing unknowingness filling all this space. which was never empty. which grows its own frightening rooms and closures, a safe prison to dream of boundlessness from. touch is thought once it keeps on going. once it drives beyond definition. upon reaching the intersection of desire, flight finds the body waiting. there are those who have tumbled over its edges, unknowing. yet even from my present farness I hear the singing of those who leapt.

rises in the urban population determining that each resident be allotted 1.6 square metres
of personal space

in blocks alternating pistachio and lettuce hue
people swam up to windows, waiting for rain, and
occasionally knocked on one another's doors
holding boxes of citrus fruit—sirens inside
sage-green paper. girls drew the linen shade
in the middle of a summer's day to keep inside
the sweet sleep of a ripe room. scent, flicker, of plums.
cardboard flats of persimmon and lychee flowered
on the sidewalk, thick between murmuring bodies
in waterproof tarps, leaned up against each other
as if complicit in some secret we would all be
so lucky to know. my mother looked for
my father in-between the pages of a newspaper,
her arms ceramic in the grey arch of afternoon.
we all sat around like we were waiting for someone
to stop by, shelling shrimp and watching television.
the bloom of plastic peonies on the sill making sure
it was invariably the right season. people weren't always
coming home at the right time, and sometimes
we spoke in a language so heavy that we passed
the words around in our hands, cupped as if to
receive new, iron, tepid, water. twenty minutes west
of the yangtze, we drank black tea spun with the thin
pink arms of chrysanthemum flowers. and when
the rains came, we looked around, bewildered and
reaching for one another, waiting for it to stop.

wealth distribution will not be considered in the economic reform

the get rich quick schemes in china
always started with two men sitting
on some battered patio over an oil-slick
of a tablecloth. the beer was cold most of
the time, but warmed quick in the grasp
of an anxious palm. you could tell
how rich a man was by how often he talked
about being poor. but back then everyone
was poor. shanghai was a firearm of a city,
grease-dark mechanics and a heavy
presence in the drawer of the day. fruit skins
draping the curb. estranged gauze of huangpu
river. pillowcases filled with plastic wrapping.
the trigger twitches—*this close* to a bicycle
for your wife, *this close* to a couple months
of rent. *this close* to cottoning the quilts
for winter and tangerines every summer night.
picking coins from pocket seams to buy
hawberries and cigarettes they sweated out
july in brick-dust. scrawling out numbers
with their fingernails. 200 yuan tomorrow
and the rest next week. cash wanders in
its own underground architecture, caverns of
paths and hollows swallowing men whole
every couple of days. they leave with unbuttoned
shirtsleeves and collars. they leave haunted
in gold. even early the past-midnight blue
coveted the skin of their wrists and necks,
soft as slow-silk, begging to be let in.
I've got two daughters, one of them says,
and the other, asleep on the table, is silent.

the coming of spring in the time of martial law

I could tell you this: marigolds are a night flower.
in the hour of my birth there were men in the streets,
some with knives and some between skin and some
peeling open buds with swollen hands trying to find
a home to hide in. my mother fingered a ripened
bowl of hot water, carving out upon its surface the lines
by which our family would occur. five tracks wavering
before being soothed to nothing. papa came in with
the hands of smoke around his mouth. a fingernail
pressed into the back of my neck. quiet now. children
rose like night-fires amidst decades in which no one spoke
above a whisper, striking the petrified days with heads
black as matches. among the dead: old hua, teacher
jian, chien-sha from the building two doors down,
cheng-yi who said the food on the mainland was better,
aunt ren and her pockets full of small oranges, young
ko and her sweet daughter who had lost teeth the day
prior. each night we soothed time as if it were newborn,
as a song about marigolds prayed through the radio
and we held death upon fingertips to count by. in those years
it was children like I that cut through our mothers spearing,
darkened already in this world by the one we are fated
to return to. worn patches in the cloth of the nation.
salt of blood in the mouth immortal as anthem. *stay still,*
just like you're dead. we whispered to hear ourselves speak.

witness

there is a long time and a time longed
for. a spectator and a combatant, the order
dreamless between them. river on pause, an especially dry
spring. departing day clearing the table of broken bread,
the light being something one turns off so as to finally sleep.
then there is someone to commit the act and someone who cries
enough. you will know once you have heard in the neverness
a promising silence. what does not happen here clasps
the entirety to its breast. what is everywhere cannot
happen here. anything short of forever is a long time,
there's never any news coming from the other side,
save for some enormous music
we all cup our ears to hear.

mong kok, october 2019

the unimaginable day was still watching
at the scene of our surrender. love was a small country
with borders made reckless. paiyang, I remember you
like this. because of the many things
that could talk, but didn't. the sky occasion.
the birdlike occasion. the starting of desire with
blindness blissfully after. and all the other things with no afters—
petrol, tear gas canisters, your face between my hands
small as if telescoped through centuries. I fell
into that open mouth like colour. the musical
collapse of ordinary things—nothing held its shape,
not glass, nor metal, nor nighttime, nor language and its conspiratorial
loneliness. when in a burst of time a new world
appears, I was still there in that warm middle
dissolving. it is so wonderful what one can do
with the unfearing knowledge of nothing
when tomorrow is a ship full to capacity
in victoria harbour scalding. paiyang, it lit
your hands into a firing thing. you will cry
because we were not able to change everything, but no—
listen, the voices are rising, and they are singing,
they are circling in a strange new formation
I've never seen before, an ocean-like current dragging
the dead out, returning back to the shore
startlingly living creatures, insatiable.

exile hong kong

when I wake I think, we've had the same dream again—
wooden board shimmering silver in scales of river fish,
pillows fat with rice, stone doorsteps, battlements of paper
wishing into the breeze. it's these thinking dreams that turn
themselves in from sleep to the wider, conscious world. this
somnabulist language we follow, grasping at its secret knowledge
until the two gripping hands of the day pull us firmly, fallingly, to
here. the cases packed in a rush to betray nothing of their origin,
door we closed gently behind us as if to comfort its splinters,
your hand that knifed the night to drain it of breath. the smokes.
the books. the photographs of my parents. in the city that looks
too much like the one we left, I saw the temple of your face
beaten gentle with all the motions of disappearing. a grave
begging to be haunted. across the sea thundering itself clean—
there we were. scattered into port, having earned somehow
this unrecognisable life. dusk separated from you in one long blue
veil of fabric, fluttering in surrender, as what we had built
solidly with hands, with work, with years collapsed noiselessly
behind us. to bear its silence we insisted aloud to one another,
we're here, even as my own voice called singingly from the past.
see—I don't know how to make a future, only the continual
swimming backwards to what the truth was then. to break
off pieces, to bring them to the present, to ensure that what
survives is not only a body, and I can look at you to see that
we've had the same dream again. that in the darkness lending
dignity to our naked shapes, we are returning to the liquid land
where the night never outlasts sleep. where, on the most distant,
nameless shores, we stay waiting, patient for ourselves to arrive.

exodus hong kong

1

listen carefully—there is land or there is water,
and a time where
you may mistake one for another.
there is day and there is night,
the only difference between them
is that a body may pass through one living
to arrive at the other no longer.

2

if by land, you will travel
through the wutong mountains. follow the path
to liantang, cross over in luofang.
bring as much food as you can. remember your name
and where you are going. you will have to say the words
as if you are not starving.

3

at the red marks of painted
stone, by the mangroves there,
I watched once a child searching
the pockets of his father
who laid perfectly still in the summer stones,
mouth filling with the rising river.

4

water is through the throat of baishizhou, across
shenzhen bay. there will be men scanning the paths,

so send your body low and fast
into the long taste of salt. the sea—
it is hong kong's. they will not take
you back from it. it is the first test of the other side's
forgiveness, to enter admitting you belong nowhere,
that you are no one.

5

dandelion, banana skins, the stems of sweet potatoes. to boil
the roots of a mountain fern for its starch. to stew grass until
a dark vegetal paste collects in the pot, and the tongue thickens
with mosses and oils. bright scream of hunger ripping the body
into constellations. famine has a smell—
sunned ashes grey-yellow in the shapeless
winter silence.

6

those that fed on barks and grasses would swell—
flesh holding impressions like clay. how seldom we think
about the substance of our bodies, unnoticed until
it must be endured, red seared skin heavy in liquid
bloom. it was better when
the people you loved stopped looking
like themselves. like watching a stranger die.

7

all this has been made by mothers into song.

8

we were arriving by the hundreds and so did not look
like people any longer. the elderly, the young, men, women, camphors,
wires, rain—all questions. it was the sea
that swam through me. I heard my own cries
coming out of another's mouth.

9

forty years later on the shenzhen side a man
carves a passage in the lobby
of a luxury hotel and travels back
forty years through it. *he was carrying me*
on his back before he fell. his hand
accusing the earth strangling
the bullet air.

10

what we knew of the new world?
barbed fence twenty kilometres long, earth-burn,
salt-lick. prying my mother's hands
hardened around a willow branch. white-eyed watchdogs
carving their lethal arc in the spine. one tests
the fit of death upon him, putting it on like fire
puts on smoke. we ran
taking what we knew with us.

11

the singing of our bodies to keep the land alive.
the singing of our bodies to keep the land alive.

the swift light against your face beautiful

green gives nothing away to the season, so I am patient
in the past. walking the strand of echoes backward, standing
on the sidewalk with the hour draped neon, candy-foil
against harbin's rendition of night. the sovereign rule
of memory—same sounds, same smells, same piquant lights
cracking like peppermint in the brims of vision, in garish
lead-blues of all-night dumpling houses, in murmurings
of girls marble-eyed, in crossed ankles drawing midair
rings as if saturnine. the age spun the city in spirals,
in mineral flame, all wax-flower tablecloths splayed
liquid, pale necks swaying curious as new strawberries,
my fingers tick in my pocket for a match-strike—-right,
one is made of all of this. there in the long field of doors
you too are catching up on days left behind, scrapping them
with a wide smile, crowned in the haze that rises from
demolished homes. amidst the poppy and paper, we meet
as if halved. our bodies glancing momentary off of streaked
glass, limbs angelic with light, palm-sized moon brought
to simmer and boil, grey steam in the binding night-skin.
it was shisidao or shuangcheng or xinlitun, then we could barely
hold the horizon, serious in the karaoke booth on min'an
street, arms coarse with dusk around one another's shoulders
during a song equating falling in love to *it's going to rain.*

even imaginary, you're the same. never singing, sitting curved
or cross-legged on the floor, bottle green of baijiu warming
like milk in elbows. the spinning strobe lights asked
their red and yellow questions over the small architecture
of your face, smiling and nodding along and vaguely filling

glasses until sight, too, simmered in ribbons of pearl-water.
harbin is a city of precipices, mountains and rivers, crossing
one crooked sidewalk, then another, past red lanterns
over a lifetime of being lit, bamboo-racked construction
sites, doorways sublime with ornament and leering byzantine
steeples. the walls ripple. I am holding that same faye wong
song parallel to breath—the one that goes, *I wonder what
season it is where you are*. it's a terrible, common knowledge
that I would be looking for you, simple as the silence always
right beneath words. but then, thinking about it, reason bleeds
into all sorts of reasons, all sorts of stories. your legs a pale path
out in front of you, half in collapse on the curb. then
the world translated its indeterminable static right there,
singing photism of understanding, everything aligning when
on occasion, I would become subject to your open eyes.

august up north always stifled with a hand over the mouth,
the sky bookmarking the city here and there with startling
moments of an opaque, weighted heat. you hated it, pulling
a seashell wrist through the stale air like needle-eye,
small fan's paper wind at your breast, interpreting in the
sieging air like a story about ardor that doesn't play to music.
I was reading it in light-patterns, in the scrapings of efflorescent
teas, in the kaleidoscope way you laughed and my thoughts
shook to pieces. the wanting to love one another for a long time
swelled, glitteringly opaquely reconisably, grew to fill the room
until we had no-where to live with it. was it more beautiful,
or all the same? there goes something sacred. reflection of you
back upon you, recollections pressing like fruit into cakes, shapes

almost singing, an unfolding as if taught by the passing of seeds.
brief star of a cigarette burning a coarse circle in the sandpaper
day, the swift light against your face beautiful. to trade one
weakness for another, what season is it? pomegranate flower
and corn-husk and winter thorn all growing—what the world
submits to the captivation of dreams. in consolation of time,
in coherence with desire, between now and then and all
improbable places, you are stepping out onto the sidewalk
ruthlessly true, mirrored from your shoulders a blaring
imprisonment of moments, a mirage one walks forever towards,
that which is invented of absence, invulnerable to disappearing.

on the last day of the heisei era

I've been reading—
small sheets of paper in the trees
upon which light writes its story of time.
the city pales with it. correspondence of morning
coming towards us in its slight envelopes
of arranged clouds. water well-known by feet.
late now, as the young half-fill their bodies,
the scenery gently shatters, manmade dusk closes,
and a nation shutters the era, thirty-years clear,
into the wide overwhelm. the past. names
for homes in this world we've interpreted
in stone-language, imagined intensely enough
towards safety. today the archipelago stills
itself innocent in definitions. tomorrow
the year, polished new, will sell us back the words
we live in. the era lifts from the black vault of the universe
like an island, like a bird staying its course, like a brush
that begs itself from the ink left to the page.
only something like belief holds itself to time, the only
object we trust more for its reflection
than its substance. its formlessness enacting a life
into everything. the patterns we call music,
the yellow sands we call seconds,
the moon's stretched leather instrument
playing across the skies.

modals of lost opportunity

the bright-out day, the rebellion of cicada song,
you said this is one of the only places in tokyo
where geishas still live.

your renegade smile
soldiering damp camellia. this moment
singular and bracketed, against all other moments.

august was a month
we measured in thunderstorm,
peeling skin from the grapevine days.

I asked, when will we arrive?
though I knew we weren't going anywhere, but
still believing in perfect questions.

sumida river had swelled
while we forgot to eat. asakusa,
a sheet of light, leaked molasses through the glass.

people are on their way to work when
you said, we'll be there soon.
even though you weren't coming.

even though we were standing on opposite sides
of the room, asking about trips we would never take,
wishing for pointless, good, weather.

the present ambers memory
into souvenir. when time argued against
merely happening, and sank deeply into shape.

bright day, cicadas, woody scent of camellia.
I thought, we are finding human ways
to kill.

the corpses of ourselves as in memory.
sumida river can't tell itself from the rain.
minutes arrived as regularly as busses.

the hour came
without sitting down. hurry and shyness precise
in theatre.

I don't want to follow, I want to change things.
but the script rises to my tongue
and ignites. the seeming cascade of what can be said.

the light will go dark as the door closes. slowly,
slowly, fever, warfare, yet nothing arrests time
as love does.

ideogram of morning

over rooftops written
        timidly into the city like
                fiction, we waited

for the day
        thickly blue
                between our teeth

pristine cotton light
        unpacking flora
                onto our limbs

chiaroscuro
        of cold juniper
                silvering wisteria

trying to start
        with our bodies
                a dialogue about colour

we bore witness
        to our own
                creation myth

and the red
        was in exactly
                the right place

you were
       a perfect compromise
              a truce on the white concrete

like someone
       all of a sudden
              thought

to build into a window
       what the light looks like
              as it is passing through

conjuring

there is no room left for disbelief, we have unsang
the songs. have stripped stones of magic. we gave
the gods power and took it back. our miracles lay
wrecked in roman columns, in the fragmented shapes
between starlight, their collapsible figures. enough proof
of faith. enough convalescence and abstract scripture,
evocations of hymn, oil-weight of paintings and their
surrendering strokes, the paths by which impossibilities
came seeking resemblance, enough ochre-rimmed
desert mirages. animal we named and battered in battles
of ordinary victory. fables retold to nothing. history
unguarded against the endless survey of capitals. we've
earned a long sleep. dreamed of its possible contours
when nearing the threshold, comfort we caught in traps,
we've given the day everything. the seige white and brave
as horizon. any morning in which we stood alongside
the words, *it has passed*. attempts at reading murmuration,
other inhuman languages, gave the inexplicable its own
holiness. distance and its hypnosis, gold and its melting
temperature, incantations waning with anise, cinnamon
smell. milk-potions and apple-carvings and oracles—
we've eaten our fill. all this to ward off the oncoming.
all of it to ward off what was already with us, the world
a question desperately seeking its own annihilation.
look around, my love. all these wild answers we've
made, and not one among them have stayed with us
through the impossible pacings of a single, waking night.

the nation of aphasia

when a writer goes missing in china
we take the red and gold paper emblems
that display the character for luck
off of our doors and paste them
over our mouths. and we go back to
the old books to learn again
what we've learned for millennia,
that you can command armies or
recompose history or traverse
from xian to changsha to mount lu
or buy a dozen eggs and none of it
will mean that your life is a promise
your country makes to you.
hong kong is a dewdrop glittering
in mid-january. we close our eyes
to take its temperature, trying to find
just the right word. the rain
only a sweet-tasting silhouette against
the gleaming skyline. late-day light
spreads a white sheet over the windows
and no one can see in. no one can see out.
still, no one ever thinks this is the day
someone will knock on the door
asking you to identify your husband
by his handwriting. how is it that
we have made a culture out of
paying a heavy price. wearing out stones
with water. chasing the sun across
the eastern front with our poems

closing in behind us like lost birds.
the gardens we do not tend. the paper
boats we do not try in the yangtze.
imagine your life is the thing
that is trapped on the tip of your tongue,
the word that is almost realized,
but you can't quite think of.

and hong kong in 2001 was always this shade of light blue

papa was a communist	mama worked in a factory
making parts for	airplanes
it wasn't quite proper	for girls to stay out all day
coming home with black oil	on the pales of fine necks
but I guess we	needed the money
the kitchen at night	shined of cigarette smoke
and bare hot-july chests	men swilling warm beer
yellow slick skin	steamed chestnut shells
grease throat laughter	glass spilling laughter
white-blue hong kong dusk	peppering our mouths
through the open	window
the balcony brimmed	with pots of laundry
stalks of lucky bamboo	red-gold ribbon curls
it was	too loud to sleep
so I curled on	papa's knee
half naked	among the sunflower seeds
overflowing ashtrays	black sesame cakes
mama putting on lipstick	over the steaming stove
occasionally threatening	to call someone's wife
and the hungry skyline	no longer fit
into the neon basin	of shing mun river
around the table	red cheeks red palms
they were taxi drivers	low-level beaucrats
shined woks	pulled rickshaws
loved their country	just enough
papa had skinny arms	skimpy black moustache
mama wore hoop earrings	a filthy mouth
sometimes I wish we	never left china
with 50,000 yuan and	a single suitcase
that they kept laughing	chain-smoking

                popping caps   off green tsingtao bottles
          doing bad impressions   of their bosses
            some teresa teng song   swaying the hot air
          a smell of smoked duck   steamed sweet potato
          in that 400 square foot   one bedroom apartment
          where no one ever got   to finish a sentence

the right to work

passage is a sudden detail in the long musical night
wherein a hand that comes in from the darkness (is it
darkness' hand?) grants—in three serrated stamps
and the nod of a pen, a clarity of exemption to where
you came. mama's long black sight airbound in relief.
papa's uneven footsteps clasping linoleum in relief.
we held one another inside coat sleeves when everything,
even countries, were echoing through us like stones
through water. all the locked outbursts of those days,
struggling wire limbs past the clasps of new-place,
grassy taste of language, weather springing up like dogs.
the hours were far too long to think in. minutes invaded
wakingly by dreams. it should be said, that the waiting
was what made us inhuman. the many corners of letters
folded down, coins stuttering in worried envelopes.
without work our hands calcified around the shape
of patience. the body in negation. when the papers came,
mama's throat, finally, loosened. a laugh almost came shiningly
there. we all smiled at one another then, papa cut an apple
into thirds. work: the sifting of the possibilities of the world
thickly through the self, into fact. papa took blocks
of shivering white tofu from door to door on a bicycle.
mama tucked shelves of lettuce into plastic mouths.
that — is what laid a brick stepping-path down middling
through the pacific. to be what one *does*. to *do* what one
can. at the eve of the passing millennium, mama was still
in her uniform. white rimmed yellow tired. the reasons
to do what one could were the same to do what one
had to. in the corners of the little room our futures stood,
watching us as one watches a storm, entering from the blue.

inheritance

my mother says about hong kong:
that wasn't your life. that was my life.
she meant the chicken boiling with anise
on the stove and the rouge pinking the edge
of the wooden spoon. the broth she raised to
her mouth to taste. she meant I couldn't taste.
too young. she put cotton over my mouth
when we went outside. air softened. it was
her life. all skins of oranges left outside
to dry and the anthemic thunder— *this is*
not the life I want for my child.
that was her life. I run into hong kong
on the street in the summertime. I say
I got off the plane and came right to see you.
she wears orange. rouge. my mother's face.
upon her so few places to lie. we sit in a cafe
in sheung wan with pink cups eating
bean cakes, and later I call my mother to say
I found our old apartment building.
that I had walked up the blue stairs
and laid my hand on the door.
hong kong a neon neckline, long hair glittering
with ship-lights, crystal balls, storm velvets.
it's her life, yet I had come, and grown
my hair, and happened upon the eastern sun
like a moon. in the morning a warm wind
moves me to the window, in quivers
of bicycle bells and water hitting pavement,
I look a long time at the woman awash

in glass. the translucency of her. the in-
betweenness of her. I think I am in control
of this liminal indecision, where nothing
ends. where ruins are rebuilt with all that
is thought to have been there.

kitchen

dressed pearls of garlic in petaline whisper,
sunlight in triangles by the cutting board
as if set to be thinly portioned and split
at the table. snapper drowsy in its dark broth,
star anise and cloves and soy in tune to fire
rhythms. gentle coax of perfume. tomatoes
in the iron pan, cinnabarian oil-ripe,
blister of a flush here and there seared
by greening chive blossom. the window, alight,
brags the late-august wind. ruffles the
room, the thin fragrance of sesame,
powdered in practiced stone. the kitchen
breathes on its own, as those who know
know—it takes a lifetime to make a meal.
cucumbers in a nest of pickled seaweed,
millet boiling for the ache of cold water,
white flesh of a bird pulsing morse in salt.
the air thickens with pouring. in her hand
chili staggered between two fingertips, digs
knuckle-deep into a bag of rice, rolling
rough marbles of peppercorn, weaving threads
the whistling steam. running sweet-grass under
the tap she was reminding herself to buy
ginger. pinned-back yellow sleeve. bread slow
in its bamboo cage, skin of the wok soft
simmering. in the kitchen years pass without
a single tender word, only a secret fire lit—
it is as her grandmother has taught her mother,
how salt teaches the falls,
and how her mother has taught her,
how iron teaches the oil,
and how she has taught me.

she says to start with cold water

late at night I think about
phoning my mother
to ask again
the proper way
to boil dumplings

when she answers
I smell pears
her hands blinking
candlelight fingers
tucking hair behind ear

in her day it is morning
planting fennel in the garden
pale arms brisk
in autumn's watercolour and
the sun sweet and green

how to locate need
amidst all else
she used to say
if you're hungry when you think of me
then I've been a good mother

I have crossed the pacific
a great number of times
now it shrinks in an instant—
in a pot of water
an enormous silence
a topography of hunger

ornithomancy

on peace boulevard some engine thunder sends
stray pavement tumbling, and in the black
dust of travel an ear is put to the ground to hear
the idiolect of footpaths, mineral-old, still
somehow speaking. language pulling knots in
the veins of the city. traffic serving its metronomic,
hypnotic purpose. beijing whose cartography
was modelled after the angelic. from gem-windows
thriving skyward, the dimmed land still gathers up
breath and smoke all in some apparition,
a city in gauze looking almost like heaven. a city
in bandages amidst its own demolition. no one
will ever again say that it's just like we never left.
what's left? camphor and paper houses.
the orange light is purple and grey and too-blue.

between the slender courtyard walls it seems
everything is counting on all this being kept
just between us. a carved sparrow trying to fly from
the pear-wood frame before its contractual, imminent
expropriation. a city clerk marries his pen
to the page and two days later mingshan houjie
is smoke and knee-deep in a red rage, ochre
brick broken from walls once laced through with
the scripture of thin broths, secrets, ceremony.
the children born on this ground were always
ancient. their stunning bodies calling backward,
backward, a lineage of soil and clay. here we
buried milk names. here we lit golden bells.

and as the razing rhythms on we lock the doors
that no longer serve their purpose of protecting.
at our feet shatters a sparrow's wings, wide
amidst chipped sprays of chrysanthemum,
toothless eaves, pale tiles scattered like petals.

taking note

for delphine

of something else kept awake by silence.
order, seldom, black words on white paper evoking
redness, a life arches from the straight arrow of proceeding
in this way of defiance. so milk rises to bread. so weather raises
the clock. the simple vehicle of sleep transporting us to tomorrow
while unmade sheets of text intimate at what can be laid to rest. I am
thinking of jacques-louis david, who drew his pale, thinking figures nude
before painting clothing on them, or how someone once told me in kindness
that having daughters is the only way to heal from the loss of a mother.
there is an ethics in all of this—in the meeting of branch and rightness
and outburst and idea, this impossible motion moving stillness. writing rain
to write the land it falls upon, to write the river fecund suddenly with storm,
and the girl running home with the collar of a jacket pulled over her head,
with the piano heard somewhere playing prelude op. 28 no. 15, because
chopin heard the rhythm of drops on his roof in a dream, and believed
himself to be drowning. therein lies it. illusion. declaration. the music.

some days come in like a bird through an open window

these days I grab at with my bare hands: the bruised, feather
down days. a shrill, unbroken song in the mouths of these days, when a
a body is barely more than steam that drowns the glass—days spent
flickering between this june and last june. waking up and saying,
which june? you look like these days. the way you used to come in,
green like whirlwind, while I was standing in the kitchen, wondering
if I've forgotten to unlatch the window. these were days of sweet rice and
homegrown ivy. cicadas. yves klein blue. bedclothes bright
as monday. or were they those days? anyway, the days know how
to fly, airsick spirals against the lampshade and the potted aloe and
all the while I was trying to figure out what my voice sounded like
while on the phone to you. the day with its velvet reach, the day tapping
its nonsense morse, the day eating and planting sunflower seeds.
I left the house with all the windows open, claiming the room
needed to be aired out. I was hoping the day would be perched
on the sill when I got back. a day with you in it. last june
the house stood with its glass mouth drinking in light summer-round,
and nothing around wasn't pretty. we ate toast in our bare feet.
the day fancy in the window's yellow square, then. these days come in
with you clipped to their mouths, and I watch them flutter against
the stucco ceiling, hung with leaden late glow, flying into rooms
attempting to go eastward, the entire world filling with their arrival.

in love as in tourism

cartography seems the strangest science today
as morning alters the fittings of the hour to form
shapes wholly new. wishing I did not know that, to leave,
it is down and right past the neighbour's potted palm,
across the street to meet the river, then ahead until
the train station crowds into view—I search the infinity
enclosed here, for any time that the future could spare.
between the words *lost* and *losing* entire worlds change
hands. where the latter informs negation the other is
duplicitous with potentialities—becoming something
even desired. suddenly one is alert to all the colours
returned to sight by merely looking, a lack of familiarity
striking the common into curiosity, just as in the folktales
in which death plays detective, the wanderer is the one
who evades the blade. it is so wonderful to not be found
but to be finding, as I discover in tokyo—whose streets
resemble labyrinth, pierced with rhododendron in spring
and thundering gingko in autumn—and remember again
when you laugh and I do not ask why. and I do not want
to know either, to whom this room belonged to before us,
or where that smell of fruit is coming from, or why a fog
rises to challenge the knowledge of places once intimately
kept. I am grateful that within you only the unknown lives,
that despite what passes between us is frail and limited
and human, we still dream of things resembling the eternal.

explain to me fate as if I were a child

how do things come up to be next
to one another. streets with no names
pressed poorly upon mountains, molasses
twilight holding the day, hip
pushed to hip during rush hour,
and old photographs leaving yellow oil
upon the new. the city-bound flocking
above the river-water, the benevolent
laying her hands on the unforgivable,
the living light that eagerly tenderizes
the dying one. how does a child
meet the future just so,
how do sprouts meet their flowers,
how do various evenings meet in the kitchen
over broths and breads. how many pairs
of hands carried fruit to this bowl.
what rhythm of music led some eyes
from here, to a place a little more
dangerous. how did we come to be with
one another, here as if enchanted, with
no more reason than two grains of sand,
and no less intoxication than two winds,
infuriated by the distance
they've both had to come.

decade

twenty yuan buys you an arms-length of cotton,
so send your eldest to the market. she has grown well,
hair cut close to the soft of her neck, downed foal-skin
in coarse shades of sifted river-sand. circle her waist
with the rough-cut edges, she is thin and so it does not
cost much. for this you are, maddeningly, guiltily, grateful.
this is a house in which not one grain of rice goes
uncounted, and the thread you use to gather the stitches
for the wedding dress, is the very same stark-yellow used
to bind bird's cabbage or pig skin. for many centuries
the women of here-place have walked from one space
of belonging to another, end upon end. it will be the same
for your girl, all raw-flush and night-dazed, for a boy
she has known only a few days. he takes her hand (is it
too thin?) and his smile opens a new taste for tenderness
in her, slightly lightening the stark solemnities of ritual—
that which all women embark on so the ground
may once again witness spring-coming. when she brings
to your side a child who weighs as much as a day's worth
of eggs, you take that round and petal-shedding round,
curled within the same cotton, singing now with new
fragrance and only a memory of its past colour. you feel
the same as you did the first time: this rapture of depth
closest to truth at the center of a body. smell of weeds,
of sweet-oil, balmy slick of sugared milk. the dress,
split back upon the seam, finds its corners in the palms
and mouths of this newborn, clipping the world with eyes
new to seeing. she will grow. slowly, as all those born
under the summer moons do, and the cotton renders

thick with her smell, her call, and it will appear red
in some places and white in others, and it will seem lace in
places and jacquard in others. it will hold teethmarks. edges
dredged in lilac laced spring, in autumn wood. in fevers.
in long rains. in the violent gnarl of impossible winter
that this land claims without any expectations of mercy,
as what is grown here was made to last. one day you will
once again stretch this breath of cotton, north to south,
measured to the length of your eldest daughter's arm,
and split from its ranges the places sweetly worn. the winds
have been strong this year, and the stalks of the land bow
low with the air, yellowed in sand. your eldest daughter
perches on the bed's edge, holding her eldest daughter.
you shear it into polite squares, as dusk measures wind
(which has breath also) and november is bitterly led
into the room. it is laid into a distinct, learned pattern,
quilted to brave the currents that heaven will concoct from
the other side of the songhua. you set aside the necessary seeds:
alliums, sunflower. the quilt will be crowded to quiet
with bodies. the child walks over. waist-height now.
sounding like your eldest when she had begged for feathers
to tie around a copper coin. it has been years since the red
was set cleanly in the cloth. longer since you were young.
water continues to be pulled from the earth. you will go blind
in your left eye, but not yet. the thread pulls the secret scents
of the past days, cleanly through the gathered stitches
of a decade. if there is such a thing as a woman's work—that.
the using of what was given, to brave what was not.

may 35th

the number four has been unutterable in china
for its homophonic resemblance to the word
meaning death. chinese is a hidden language
even as it is spoken, seeking out new homes
in which we may pull unlined, shining cloth
over the same battered bodies. contrary to what
many have believed, when a skyscraper is built
over a graveyard, nothing happens—the contract
does not allow for haunting. there are new names
to learn. 63+1. 8 squared. 65-1. that day, this day.
today. yesterday. the names belonging to the dead
take turns in the mouths of the living, tenants
excavated from the ravage. in hopes that what we say
will be understood tomorrow, we skip the number
four. in the colossal desert of muxidi few bulbs
laden the darkness in strange clothing, casting
confessions onto the plainclothes police
upon whose tongue *memorial* is *construction*. so it is
we say *construction* and *memorial* is born again.
putting our language to sleep the way a mother seeks
a last scrap of fabric for the mouth of an ageless child.
to say that victory is the abandonment of silence
would mean we had something to replace silence with.
even death seeks transformation, onward, urgent,
writhing itself inside so many given names.

only in silent shadows and in dreams

how externalities are internalities resolved—
even as the sparrow, bored with attempts at definition,
skips away, leaving small alphabet footprints
in the margined crunch of january snow.
there are projections of language, captive amidst
conversation when suddenly things are possible
in that intimately orange colour of possibility,
and in the violence of idea comes a perfect counterpart,
blown in from a lifetime of foliage, streets,
sorrow, and solace. then even the impossibly vain moon
sits in a thrall, for its decadent, unhappy yellow
is made exactly real by the resemblance to the nile
as you saw it once, outlined in the pencil of september—
like this the mind has its own methods for multiplying,
possessive even of nights that have never been,
careless over the ones that have, and standing
chatting under the window of the transient
pleading for permanence. relief that we are here
exchanging upon the market of divine illusion
what's inside for what's not, in this day seeping broken
here and there with forgetting. the fractures we fill in
golden with recollection, for what else stands a chance
on the battlegrounds of daily-things—dictatorial traffic lights
and wilting stalks under supermarket glare—if not
a fragrance, a piece of music, a strong-handed colour,
making its way from the submerged boats of history
roaringly into the present, joining instant to instant
the unknowing world with the spacious persistence
of a mind in pairs. casing the darkness, growing its texture,
compelling it to the page, granting it visible.

speak

he wrote me a letter from beijing.

there are a lot of nights, in one stroke, that I don't remember, a lot of nights
where dark was a name and hurry was a couple hours and love was the spit
        at the bottom of a bottle of water

breathing timed by the smoking of a cigarette
wishing to disappear altogether is wishing to disappear intact
        not in pieces

hu yaobang had died. the city was a fever. you couldn't get a sense of it.
sometimes the whole city felt as though it was one drop of water in a glass,
and sometimes it ran itself into rivers.

nights, these green nights, green nights hot underneath clothes, nights
hardening mouths around the shapes of words, wandering qianmen
dashilan, the alleyways of langfang where shadows slowly shift in latent
puppetshows of incidents and dreams, incidents and intentions
closing in on something that might be a stranger whose skin no longer fits
or a thousand strangers dissolving into public dreaming

he asked me if I would rather stand with my back to something
or face it.

it wasn't until later that these nights would grow stiff
with morning-things. leftovers from four knuckles on the back of your neck
hands grasping glass then grasping air then grasping a light that breaks like foil
it first takes a silence, and then it will take many, many years of noise

june and its wooden stations parsing the stops between an original
and its endless echoes. papers courageous with calligraphy
girls in filthy dresses dragging at the ankles of soldiers, moving as one
bodies blue and white bruising the darkness
          horizonal pauses

tomorrow a committee will come and collect the parts
handful of teeth, bayonet, pair of shoes flattened into the ground
many buckets of water are thrown along the hallway of the hospital

I thought that they would grab him and lock him up for twenty years. I said okay,
you can keep him if you have to. he'll still be my son after twenty years.
I never thought of a body as a precipice.

the summer we had been given
to meet all the summers to come
nights, I wake up with black powder in my mouth
how did I get here in my mouth

speak, again

we didn't know our names
until we heard it in their mouths
we didn't know what we loved
until we were summoned to guard it

in beijing the young writers ask me why people always want to talk about censorship

do they think we have nothing to say
except to mourn. why do you ask me to explain
the reasons I write despite—what do you expect
me to say? look: the concentric traffic of beijing protects
its heart. I have never, and will never throw a stone.
forbidden words have no superiority over
the words we are given.
there are more pressing things, like the price
of peaches. if quiet is such a sin where else would
we go to think. to own language is to entrap it.
no one has ever owned language.
chinese people know the frailty
of words. how it changes mouth to mouth.
there is very little time to spend thinking about
what the government is up to.
how deceptive surfaces are. most people look to the ocean
to see only themselves.
were you not given words and limits by which
to use them?
it is not fear that stops us, it's boredom.
I have no patience to explain to others
what it is we have lived through.
are living through.
before we learned to be ashamed
or furious we had to first learn to live.
why do they talk about us as if we are dying
when we are living and loudly at that.

the emperor and I dream of immortality

I know there are those who know where summer goes
                            but I am not among them
when leaves are yellow as dandelion and suspended flutes
        of daffodil
        when what falls does not make anything like music
and chrysanthemums rise tingling their many arms
it is all upwards or below while I am somewhere inside
                    as the breeze lifts the heavy sleeves
                    slow against the skin in dreadful august
        and it feels good
        I am tired

it is autumn in the city where the emperor strolls by
waving with practiced, solemn joy
                        I'm thinking of the six thousand children
                        who sailed with xu fu in search of immortality
                        during this the most ghostly of months
                        which puts everything back in array
                        and everybody doing the living lives with
                        the obvious secrets defeat keeps to itself

tell me faced with the sea how does one confuse dreaming from eternity
                        even if in the tide a thousand glinting beasts ignited
                        a thousand archers would be sent after them
        for living forever would mean not the end of fear
        but a lifetime of it and therefore a lifetime carved
        into the minds of all fearing beings which is to say
                            all beings and that
                    is what the qin emperor knew
        when the first stones were laid in what would become
                        the great wall of china

when xu fu boarded the great ship strewn with the tapestries
with cartographies of mountains warped with alchemic legends
he scanned the horizon to convince himself of endlessness
                              which we know by its daily name
                          circuity

    there was no empress during the qin dynasty
                      it is said that the emperor became convinced
            that the love of a woman corrupted the simple decisions
                                      of the man who loves power
            and thus he brought scraps of girls forth along the brick
            under the bronze glances of spirals of diamonds
            and into the dark clearing of his swollen legs
                              their noiseless shackles dragging
                          the skin from their sapling limbs
        the bones of chinese women outweigh the great wall
        in the same immeasurable quality of territory

today the yellow perfect yellow varying green gold yellow leaf
            dropped ruined as last light onto my shoulders
                                  and I was full of being hunted
        and I too would have stepped onto the planks of the ship
        roaring ship pursuing the cure for death
        shiningly red for the sake of luck
                  in stifling autumn seeping from its edges

        I would slip off
            on the wide search for days without end
but when I imagine myself I do not see a warrior
xu fu with furrowed brow and hems dipped in gold
I do not see a child pitched overboard as a promise for the future
            pure child with roses stained onto the skin by leeches

I do not see myself
                    in the grand proclamations of history

the emperor had called one of his most beautiful women to him
                    she had stood bare drenched in sight
          and upon the new page of her body was written
          the vision of everlasting youth
                         the known source of great fear
     on blood-strands he hung the script of a dynasty
     envisioned to last ten thousand years
     and the place in the sky where xu fu's ship disappeared
               is marked by a small shallow deft
                    where days struggle out
  from beneath the small hands of the night

in the palace chrysanthemums are soaked into the wine
poured into a mouth sip after sip by knotted hands

                         the bodies of women whipped into leather
                    and metals tempted into shapes of swallows
          were amongst the many cures for death

in twenty years I will be forty nine years old
the age of the qin emperor when he died
bribed from life by a mercury pill
clutching china in spinning palms
 and a hundred rivers were embedded in his tomb
          alongside massacred soft heaps of women
               by which the emperor insured his rest

                    if I can I would like to live a long time
eternal going in all wrong directions and as far as imagining

even during the arrows of storm that ensnarl
the rims of these years to plunge them deep into the earth
                         living earth from which the buried call to us
                         the disarmed and torn call to us
                         with similar designs of immortality
              hatched by men who made death bearable by convincing
              their desires deep into the solid bodies of women
if living long is an act of vengeance then I am not so righteous
     as to deprive myself and if it is a culmination of fear
     then yes I am afraid almost all of the time
                    of never becoming quite deserving
                    to be a woman who somehow lives

during the qin dynasty it is possible the days were longer
measured by counts of torrent and sand and the waving figure
of a hand which beckons you to come
                              to sing to dance to part your lips
possible that those relentless days provoked the first instance
of time that seemed indestructible

              autumn's gorgeous strangling yellow fingers
              portioning age-shaped bruises along a nation
              unified by the first emperor
              every single crevice in the great wall of china strains
echoing backwards forwards along the greatest physical monument ever built
                    in the name of terror and its disparate shapes
                         all resembling so closely
                         visions of eternal life

looking twice

in a green walk-up behind the sumida river, there's
a mattress on the floor, supplied in ivy. and through a window
no one can see into, there are hours, carved from a night
translucent. inside them, a room where, between 4am
and your shoulder, I saw yellow. there, a day threaded
through the simple gaze of other days in succession. some-
-how making its way here, again. along the bank a girl
plucks a dark round from the gathered grapes, sneaking one.
small squares in mid-air glared bright white
when someone turned a light on inside of them.
I walked through the rhododendron and remembered
the skin of your arm warm and strong between my teeth.
despite knowing that the only eternities are those slipped
into the remote catalog of forgotten things, I found myself
at the base of a green building. looking up. seeking that most
difficult thing—not resurrection, something freer. life unbound
from the circumstances of its birth. a memory that stands up
without its frame. single room withholding the elapse of years
holding still the gentle matters of love, as if a dream
had finally—after a terrible struggle—escaped from the mind.

search by no light

by   the antibesian waters
of tokyo   bay
I   search   my body
    by   no   light

learning   and naming
what   I alone   can touch
leather   pearl
    paper   silver

where   and how
within   me   contains
artillery
    who put it there   why

the moon   admitted
courting   river birches
light   does not blanch
    hand   prints   water   stains

upon   the skin
past   touches   lie
powdered
    sifted   and   merging

the secret taste
the   bullet   rising
my creation myth
    has   no tale of falling

the dictionary of desire

nothing can fix the finite which lies between the two infinities that enclose and flee from it.
—blaise pascal

horizontals—
wide waste of water. burnt-out television fragrance, smoking in absence,
peonies and the word peony. even images get turned around if we try to find
and name unnamable things. the tongue's full pink plate of words. what
do you see, when you picture static? if appetite is what takes the air from

causality—
beginning with a clean shearing blade down the middle. so aristophanes
claimed we wander the earth as searching halves. I grew up under the fear of
earthquakes. knowing what happens when separate, powerful bodies come,
as in fascination, as in momentum, as in defying the fact of edges, to meet

fiction—
the knowledge of green is told in the language of trees. the knowledge of hunger
is told in hunger. to take in the generous way the night takes in the land,
all of it, one mouthful. to fall is always to move through something that
hasn't taken place yet, one digs with their body a tunnel for the following

heaven—
a painted glove hitting the canvas, blue blue detonations. always the deep
pool of colour at the centre of impact, like the beginning of meaning was
meanings singular. the fault is to have looked at the world as how it has been
made, instead of how it has been imagined. dislocation of blue by a single

chorus—

if only transposition were enough. if we were for even a second free of our
helpless powers of change. in the pulse of two fingers held to the throat lay
a dark pulsing morse of yes. I ran, yes I ran, towards the cannibal light breaking
teeth on the day, like fire struggling to be born under all that continent, all

extent—

slide pins into the wings of your longing. study what makes it historical. eye
which takes emptiness as a place to rest, like when someone told me, in language
I did not understand, that not understanding was also a method we've found to
speak into one another. to send a mind outwards because it is safer there than

free—

slow purple braids of wisteria pouting honey into spring's crepe collars, my
musical-wild, sonnet-laced mirror image holding out the hidden. we were
sitting underneath the eucalyptus, the heat had settled like a cat in the soft
inner nods of elbows. how my body learned the language of desire. word by

the man I love ran off with everything except my poems

there was a thought hanging like a trick of light on the door
as if it could fall at any second. we knew if it fell
it would make a sound like water. the thought communicated
with its wayward tracings that it did not know to whom
it should return. the door was a fiction of the thought,
who had changed it from nothing to have something
to hang to. my hair is yellow in the fiction. then it is black
almost as fact. your hair is walnut in the photograph,
until fact throws a wild light upon it. doors are a fact
of their swinging, and water has noiseless ways of
entering the room. your eyes are what filled the doorway
to pieces. in a book about love gertrude stein
says that her portrait from picasso is the only reproduction
which is always I. I, I want to take I, back from I. from
your eye of doors which lead powerfully into silence,
and an illegible, animal approach of resemblance.
the immortality desire inflicts is the perpetual living-on
of somewhere other, just as a door can only ever be
open or closed, never neither. just as fictions come to live
side by side with fact, and hair greys sometimes in sleeping.
the days all rest around in halves like oranges,
I, and I, and I laying between them, being as much someone
as they are anyone.

eve on a one night stand

paradise lost, shinjuku on thursday nights,
angel forms of gold warping ordinary shame
into ripe cloying pleasures. whiskey
in glasses, then in tall metal cylinders, then
bitterly aluminum cans, spiced nuts
and untouched rice. midnight revels
even as the clock strikes past it. what light—
two packs of cigarettes and one match
between them. I touched the fruit, and knew
it rotten. *shame, the last of evils.* yet I crossed
nothing in divinity, and the non-possessed
never believe in possession. there was
the smell of sex before the suggestion
of it; the unripe aroma of circumstantial
intimacy. before knowing better, knowing
wanting. in a love hotel snake-headed
through kabukicho I moved beneath
a man who refused to say his real name.
I said mine, anyway, which seemed to work
at holding me to my body for a little while,
a little while when I was not mind nor speech
nor idea, but only glancingly, my body,
without questions. he picked one of my hairs
from his chest and let it fall to the floor. I reached
for a fig leaf. moments in which you become
a stranger to yourself always happen
with someone else, when without knowing
you adjust to their methods, and in this bloodletting
an understanding is meant to be born.
at seven in the morning we dressed. I brushed
my teeth with the disposable toothbrush
and single-serving portions of toothpaste and

the high winds worse within. sex is no sin
and no absolution. I only knew I had the desire
to wander, and that I had said yes
when perhaps I had meant to say no
but not sure. it is not simple to know
wanting when wanting bleeds, is human
one moment and hollow the next. the air
was due to be gentler and I stretched
into the very edges of my body
reluctantly, testing its fit, its weight. purity
seemed a chokehold of virtue, *without thorn
the rose.* I watched the man with no name
cross the street and descend into
the mouth of shinjuku station as if it was
heaven's gate. girls in pairs twisting ankles
on the long orange curb, shorn stalks
of yellow flowers, smudge of wine. *in such
abundance lies our choice.* it was breakfast time
and I was going to scream, but I got on the train
instead. the earth arched once again
towards the blank face of a strange world.
I counted reflections in the glass
that so resembled the sky as I arrived
closer to myself, on my solitary way.

montreal

baked brick, dark bread,
breath sinking into a hot, grey bath when
caught in smoke between compartments
on the metro. pink lights from
the townhouse on rue de rushbrooke
blinking away as the sky tries to dark. stillness
losing out, always, to movement.
chequered tile, white corduroy,
men who smell exactly like
their animal selves eating dollar-seventy
hamburgers out of wax paper. the radio
doesn't work, but someone's playing
billie holiday upstairs, and someone else's hearing it,
and it sounds right, being so far away.
music rigid and counter-history in a night
that is not. a night that is neat in the parade
of nights. the streets are full of garbage. laundry
yellow and falling out of the sky like flowers.
a small boy walks and walks and walks along charlevoix
without coming across a single
other person.

montreal II

I was getting lost all the time so I had to pick up smoking. I mean with a cigarette you could stand on the side of the street and lean up against the black haunt of wrought iron or the paintingly green staircases of august foliage or the parking meter and you could wait. you could let the world demonstrate its order to you, all the while looking as though you belonged in it, in the era of perfect maps and imperfect memory. this is only one of the minor intersections between pleasure and powerlessness. when the streets stop making sense at least your body has to. at least your wanting has to. the soft white circles of paper, the darkly acid smell, the small fire one always carries, if not in the pocket then in a pouch with mints and safety pins. to say I am lost is to find the I. the *I* that uses all the breath in the body to say *where*. I'd like to think I've built a new theory, fire by small fire, of wayfinding. to get close enough to something that you fold it into your mouth. take it. I mean take a left. I mean take what's left. everything recognised in the distance turns out to be a stop you have to make yourself. to consume something in the brief shift of an interruption. how new, each time. to get near that sense of nothing fitting. how lucky to not fall in it.

montreal III

she said to him   I mean you've been saying forever about
                             not wanting to stay in one place your whole life

I know
I just worry

                    that day the churches were full and if you knew
                    then you knew about the many candles being lit
                    in the ancient silence, of gold lowering idle
                    softness in the dark. it happens every handful
                    of years, when certain absences tear into the material of
                    common, shared landscapes with its singular, capillary
                    system. the grief which is unable to be faced, for it has no
                    sides and no shape, only the ability to grab onto the vehicle
                    of any body to make its own, unbridled, way.

        this time it was a boy. worse. a very young boy.

tomorrow   she said   tomorrow   in the future   that's when
the truck will come   and we'll get all these boxes in the truck
and then it's just you   and then you can go

he put his hand on her leg   she laid her forehead on his arm
it's like this that an afternoon is built piece by piece and
nothing simply happens

two months ago, eric, a three-year-old living in ahuntsic-cartierville
built a house of spare wooden blocks—rescued from the detritus
of never-completed neighbourhood projects, and sanded down to
round edges by his father. the house had a door standing slightly
ajar, which struck the detective as odd, for it seemed a bit advanced
considering the architect's age.

          and then I'll come with you
          she said
          later   when I can

     after they touch they look out the window together
the sky which tells more than the clock   the limp conifers
small animal   crossing the street like a sound
     custard sunset of late autumn
          inviting night in like a guest

     some people at the church want to know who
     hasn't shown up. it matters—no, listen, it matters—
     who does or does not show up to these things. in
     another room the children are gathered with crayons
     and chocolate cookies and rectangle stickers marked
     with names. it also matters that they are not where
     the candlelight, pointing upward in daggers, can
     touch them. no. candles should remain for children
     objects of wishful symmetry. birthdays. hannukahs.
     not floating like this in seeming nothing over a body.

there are deals you can make with the night
you can trade the body of a man you love into it
he will be sent a long way down
     the way wind sends down grass-seeds along riverbeds
and you will look after him with your eyes searching the dark
     like a key

     and in return you will feel that
     you understand what leaving looks like

the janitor cleaning the church that night stays an hour later
than usual   and feels the same gladness to be alone
in the presence of lightning   or an angel
                    depending on the night
with the wax pooled in thick meaty circles on the altar
and the thin citrus-poison smell of the polish
and the silence shaking in the humming black
                    like a cane for the blind

montreal IV

G—

        no light on but the one in the kitchen
is how I'm writing to you. I like the telephone but
this feels better. when you read these words the sounds
you hear will have been translated through my body
first.

        yesterday I received my passport in the mail.
the photograph is a ghost, but recognisable, features
and all of their exclusion. I think the person in the picture
looks like someone who never smiles, so you will not say
she looks like me.

but a precious object nonetheless. you know how you
say—it is strange, how paper traps things. this document
is where my whole life lies, an answer to the questions
of history, like a small death in amber.

                     as soon as I can
I will send more money. it depends on the weather, my head.
sometimes they'll make me leave as soon as I arrive
because they want the girls with no papers to work more.

it is very strange that the world I live in is still connnected
to yours. it feels as though by a very thin strand on which
only a letter will fit. a voice feels too volatile. too heavy.

the fruit is very different. apples sharp and pears
soft. they're green—sweet green or grain green, with small
sprays of brown markings that remind me of the pattern
lace on your thigh.

I am learning english
from the radio. today I heard a very funny phrase:
alternate version of events. it means if something happens,
the story someone tells about it can be equally as true
as fact. as if facts are being suspended in the air on
puppet strings of people telling. doesn't that sound
like our whole lives?

winters here
are supposedly as hard as the ones back home. void
and white and small in hours. but they do not build
gardens from the ice.

I'm also sending my recipe
for chicken and ginseng soup. make it, and drink
when it's too hot as I would do. one long pour of
warmness. sometimes a fog descends and eats up
the city in chunks. one day it will part and I will
see you.

yours, from here,
—S

montreal V

the truth is that I tell the truth in the first half of my life
so I can lie in the last. I said *solemnly swear*, said *july*, said
montreal. it is the moving away of time to seem wider,
and the reducing of the day so it can be made usable.

the grace of echo—that she is not a body but a gallery
of infinities. the drawing of a line between myself and nowhere.
one refuses to be made into statue, choosing instead
nothingness. fictions. when you can't see the moon, that's when

you know—she is being born away from herself.

to talk with you

I call you because it is summer where you are,
so it is a simple act by which time,
and distance, and all other infallible things
are defeated. where did I read that october
has always belonged to poets. where
do we go after arrival in this surviving month,
when the country sheds its coloured skirts
in admittance of finality. streets pursued
in stutters of autumn roses, the yellow-cast
gingko, collapsed foliage, papered pathways,
thinned cherry blossom reaching their sweet
smelling skeletons toward one another across
the shallow river. among them I feel the pull
of your midday sun, unbroken and stranded
in my voice, saying things to you, sounding off
the shattered waters. on my side of the earth
grey is blown gentle into the stony air. say this
is a poem I wrote with your interior, where
this love between women remedied the
long parenthesis of failures: ours, the world's.
your noon and my evening congregated,
touched. the wind stops to hear us speak.

love poem in the way of a late game of scrabble

since from incoherence we are to distinguish
language. fragments of which we did not create
but feel still somehow responsible for possessing,
the luminous homing-down of letters in the right
condolences of a word—unrimmed darknesses answered
like time by minutes. I've thought about it in the odd night,
facing the empty page, counting on dreamwork and creases
to scatter forward in the same senseless order of wooden
tiles, to make what I have to say about you make sense.
how easily language comes to us, then how difficult
to sculpt this substance into the broad positions of living,
safe consonances on a splayed piece of cardboard
the cruel resolution to what I have tried to do with
all these pieces of sentences. all these pieces that are not ruins.
you are studying the row of neat squares before you,
unsmiling. you are writing figures in mid-air, in dissolution,
in reformation. these sentiments. these ideas coerced
by this world that insists towards order. I wish I knew
a better way. looking at you, the hair by your ears curled
in cirrus shapes. your imbalanced mouth which strands
me on my body of wanting. the shape of love is a line,
that which everything hangs upon and nothing rests,
but the shape of the whole world faces us in squares.
the branching architecture of our own private definitions
within which speaking and silence are holding each other.

returning to paros

the great moons of history coalesce
upon the now-sky, the middle of here

an ocean. magritte moon. hiroshige moon.
o'keeffe, miró, hopper. swimming in the fine

white cloth that evening now touches,
stunned. I see in the figuring air what

has gathered within it—running-late august
with the bright brittle of walnuts, crumbling olive

breads, broad swords of geranium, weaving
our brined language into the wind, wearing

salt into the linen, an arrival at each clock
a little later. I stand here with scraps for

the restless animal of memory, to resemble less
someone waiting. the meltemi has swept

the inner shore free of direction
since I began counting days, since even blue

is differently blue, and I love you differently
in the no longer. with the aegean, anemone,

wet wordlessness. with wind stirring the edges
of body into night. you came back also, only

no longer able to change. and I hold to it.
I speak. between wildflowers domesticated

in painted jars, the sky can be felt escaping
in any direction. jagged island edges

maddening to draw. impossible to imagine.
this must be the true terror, then,

that the dead bestows upon us—that they will
come back to find us in need of them still,

stranded on the long coast of patience,
pointing at what used to be, and saying *could.*

always the clock, always the corridor, always the staircase

after wong kar wai's in the mood for love

I am calling something by its name — it's time. that
which passes for nothing other. save for perhaps the surface,
which things rise to meet.

> imagine how we are seen
> opening doors in ourselves.
> ledges scaled to look upon
> one another awhile. willing plates
> to shift under the continent
> of desire, for an island to rise.

what does my voice do, but send me to you, in pieces?

a qipao is made with the woman's body imagined,
so one only has to gather herself for its form. to clear
the conscience of a double nature, she never takes
it off. darkens it as air does the fruit. as ellipsis does
the sentence.

> she is the same seen in light as in shadow
> still it is sight that translates her into fire.

down the hall
    across the table
        back of a taxi
           in a doorway

the world was lived to fill. those who abstain know
something that you and I do not — wanting in itself
is hollow, mere outline tracing a body on dissolving
paper. we are perfect thinking of the other, warm
of each other, clutching at the air as if it were dark.

meanwhile our old habits are looking around
curious to know who will come to fill them.
                    my helpless papers, your tray
                    of limelit pigments and oils.
objects as the only hope of returning to oneself.

to create a frame of reference, it was thin-coat summer,
days dropping as if playing dead, we blinked them away
easy as eyelids. red silk, green glass, black leather, wood.

hall   table   taxi   doorway

it was what could be changed yet
                              into early and late.

tourniquet in body in memory, one has to be ancient
to live this life. the now as if having already been
a thousand times. I hear the stifled desperation
of the future trying to fight its way into the present,
I put my hand over her mouth. I say—let me.

                              I am extending
                              passing over
                              calling you
                              falling sleep
for answer in a place where there is not yet a question.

we do not rest at the edge
nor the center of any recollection,

                                     but hover above
                                     seeking downward.

the capacity of beauty to resist idea. she moves as if
he is watching her — she enters him, watching herself.
tilt your head ninety degrees, and the standing to face
comes newly to be implicated in the descending
moment of embrace. free is having no ground
to stand upon.

coffee, silver,
shorn head of dark hair, warm tremble of a round mouth.
air irrevocably shaped to hold you there, *in* place.

space is defined by the open decisions of separation.
hall table taxi doorway. empty is somewhere to say yes in.

how to tell—shine a light there. something will either
appear, or disappear.

I reach for you across this.

southward

green room. yellow clockwork. the road
curves into lake and the lake pleads itself over
to become land. seeds touch and immediately
become fruit. in hanoi youth alternates like
mango season, rising and dropping
and shining as it ripens. early in the morning
before the dreamy heat men sit low
on plastic stools, in doorless coffee houses,
smoking filterless cigarettes, the girls in twos
and threes on motorbikes shield their wrists
from the blaze. newspapers wrapped around
the handles of pots. bread golden inside
glass boxes. street hung with tapestries
of leaves and stove-smoke, sun sweeping the day
clean of night, and the ground tastes of bones,
of orange-rind. if it is the role of the living
to track history to the present, then it is here
we find, with morning noises, violent films,
plastic carnations, the agony of definition.
in homes dressed up pink and blue
for the eternal summer, time is sung
by lamp-jewelled dragonflies and palm-leaf
winds, by candles lit to mothers and by whatever
will pass. devour the vine, the bicycles,
the butter avocados. thickly swallow the boys with
flat and brown feet, the roofs shadowed
with lanterns at dusk, rice paper pinched
into white roses. to find where need begins,
look for the places where nothing dies,
for the ways by which holy places are made

holier. where the wooden boats spoon
up the waters and children in tank tops
eat sandwiches, where long pages are written
between pillars precise as teeth.

the gallery of distances

simply we found that the world had grown long and was old,
and with that the talking stammered to nothing. such quiet.
a quiet thick and lavender as the vegetal perfume of night-patterns,
taking turns to ride these spokes of memory, oscillating silver.
looking around everything is on time. by which I mean everything
rests atop of time, which is now writhing and shaking frantically,
a shadow struggling to get out of the light and back into the dark,
it is said that true silence makes you lose your mind, but it's
distance that does it for me—how we explain the inexplicable
by only referring to the nature of things. here, late summer steals
into available image, taking colours of unreal sheen, dabbing them
as picture. the lambsgrass, the bold-minded dandelion, the funny violet,
and so on until the hills are gratified with its mélange, and claps
two branches to welcome the evening. it has become the eighth month
of a very long year, and one thinks now of more generous years past
that had felt so easy to wander away from, as the world then was not
so dependent on being hoped on. but of course something else is taking
place. the last sun luxuriates in the criss-cross between tiles when a friend
calls me to tell of another vague death that has occurred somewhere
not quite out of reach, and between the breathing pauses I see
a small bird who has just left her perch swiftly turn back and land again,
almost as if the whole business of flying had suddenly begun to terrify.

what language we have is used to tell the future

five hundred marks towards the east
lies the mountain named danxue
whirled-veined with minerals and jades
chasmic obsidian and bittersweet opals
water flows there into the mouth of the bohai
and then onward to become all waters
in this mountain lives a bright-bird
whose figure resembles briefly other birds
though along its body are many-coloured feathers
which do not catch the light so much as contain it
it is called for wind and for flame
as within one eternity contains the other
phoenix—its body is written everywhere of names
that we did not create but were given
its forehead the character for goodness
its wings the character for breath
its back the character for ceremony
its chest the character for kindness
its stomach the character for verity
though it feeds from the ground as other birds do
it knows little of hunger
as hunger is a human frailty that morphs
all too easily into greed
should you happen to glimpse it even once, my love
from across the caverns of salt and pillow-lily
we will have peace and all those silly pleasures
and it shall seem something like fate

all light atop the mountain is soft light
wild orchids sparrow grasses rabbit flower
long mutable landscape of the warring states
twisted in shapes distinct and murderous
here we learn our names by repetition
speaking first into a celestial nothingness
so that in the deep eye of the world
there we were glinting
weaving nameless stems into the clothes of our children
inquiring waters to learn the directions of harvest
and poetry was something the wind wrote
in the cursive, dusty language of poor weather
we told stories that grasped at their own edges
with only beginnings and no endings
for history was in the startling middle of its creation and
we shared it as we shared coal and rain
when we bid goodbye to our men
we did not know that we had become a country
nor that the red thing called marvel
could turn into the red thing called violence
so when upon hearing the story of peace
a man sets out with blades and flint
the blind night holding close the blind rain
we did not look into the distance
to send the myth to its ending
for the only thing plenty in this world are stories
and the time it has taken to tell them

details escape

returning to the place where memory goes
which resembles most closely the stagger of stones
needling the hem of land at minoura's feet
water work of the inland sea already interlocking past

I think I had to take more than one deep breath
to commiserate with the animal we named silence
beaten under depths rest good fruit car crashes
invented grandmothers more sunrises than reality

who is the owner of unremembered moments
would they open their great book
if I stood
at the door
and begged?

Made in the USA
Middletown, DE
16 September 2023

38512203R00057